I Was There

by

Bob Hope

COMPILED AND EDITED BY
WARD GRANT

Dedication

This book is dedicated to the American GI - and the men and women of the Allied forces of World War II and to those who served so valiantly on the home front, especially my wife, Dolores - who kept the home fires burning, tended the kids and weeded my victory garden.

B.H.

INTRODUCTION

In the entire history of show business, no individual has travelled so far - so often - to entertain so many, as Bob Hope.

To the American GI and all the men and women serving in the armed forces of the free world, Bob was the ultimate road warrior. For fifty years Hope travelled the globe entertaining troops in combat zones and on lonely duty far from home.

The tradition, the legend of Hope and the GI, started in 1941 when the country was still at peace. During World War II, on remote airfields, aboard ships at sea, at sub-zero Alaskan outposts, one piece of scuttlebutt persisted: "Bob Hope is coming."

The reports of these visits were well chronicled at that time: *Time Magazine* (Sept. 20, 1943) elevated Hope above the dozen or so major entertainers touring the war zones. He was labelled as a legend, representing "measurable qualities in a mystical blend" and had developed, to the delight of millions of people, into an American folk figure:

...thanks to his vibrant averageness, Hope is any healthy, cocky, capering American. He is a guy who livens up the summer hotel, makes things hum at the corset convention, keeps a coachful of passengers laughing for an hour while the train is stalled. With his ski-slide nose and matching chin, he looks funny but he also looks normal, even personable.

And although he hugs the limelight with a showman's depthless ego, in Hope himself is a hunger to reach people as a human being. For a performer who scarcely takes time out to live, perhaps it is the only way of being one."

Bob Hope had a different perspective. He called himself "the longest delivery Chicken Delight ever made."

Actor Burgess Meredith, who served as Director of the USO in Great Britain, wrote in a letter to Paulette Goddard:

The most wonderful thing about England right now is Bob Hope. The boys in camp stand in the rain, they crowd into halls so close you can't breathe, just to see him. He is tireless and funny, and full of responsibility, too, although he carries it lightly and gaily. There isn't a hospital ward that he hasn't dropped into and given a show; there isn't a small unit anywhere that isn't either talking about his jokes or anticipating them. What a gift laughter is! Hope proves it.

Ernie Pyle, *New York World Telegram* wrote:

I was in two different cities with (the Hope troupe) during air raids and I will testify that they were horrifying raids. It isn't often that a bomb falls close enough that you can hear it whistle. But when you can hear a whole stick of them whistling at once, then it's time to get weak all over and start sweating. The Hope troupe can describe that ghastly sound...

JOHN STEINBECK, WRITING FOR THE *New York Herald Tribune*, SAW HOPE AS A CLOWN-HERO TO THE GI:

When the time for recognition of service to the nation in war time comes to be considered, Bob Hope should be high on the list...

He has caught the soldier's imagination. He gets laughter wherever he goes from men who need laughter...It is hard to overestimate the importance of this thing and the responsibility involved. The battalion of men who are moving half-tracks from one place to another, doing a job that gets no headlines, no public notice, and yet must be done if there is to be a victory, are forgotten. But Hope is in the country. Will he come to them or won't he? And then one day they get the notice that he is coming. Then they feel remembered.

The man, in some way, has become a bridge. This man drives himself and is driven. It is impossible to see how he can do so much, can cover so much ground, can work so hard and be so effective. There's a man. There is really a man.

WARD GRANT

With Ernie Pyle at Palermo, Sicily, 1943.

PREFACE

I was there... I SAW YOUR SONS AND YOUR HUSBANDS, YOUR BROTHERS AND YOUR SWEETHEARTS.

I SAW HOW THEY WORKED, PLAYED, FOUGHT, AND LIVED. I SAW SOME OF THEM DIE. I SAW MORE COURAGE, MORE GOOD HUMOR IN THE FACE OF DISCOMFORT, MORE LOVE IN AN ERA OF HATE, AND MORE DEVOTION TO DUTY THAN COULD EXIST UNDER TYRANNY.

AND I CAME BACK TO FIND PEOPLE EXULTING OVER THE THOUSAND-PLANE RAIDS OVER GERMANY... AND SAYING HOW WONDERFUL THEY WERE! THOSE PEOPLE NEVER WATCHED THE FACE OF A PILOT AS HE READ A BULLETIN BOARD AND SAW HIS BUDDY MARKED UP MISSING. THOSE THOUSAND-PLANE RAIDS WERE WONDERFUL ONLY BECAUSE OF THE COURAGE AND SPIRIT OF THE MEN WHO MADE THEM POSSIBLE.

UNTIL A LOT MORE OF US REALIZE WHAT OUR MEN WENT THROUGH IN PLANES AND TANKS, IN LANDING BARGES AND ON FOOT IN THE MUD, DESERT, AND ON THE BEACHES IT WILL ALWAYS BE TOUGH TO TALK TO THE MEN COMING BACK.

I DIDN'T SEE IT ALL. AND GOD KNOWS I DIDN'T DO ANY FIGHTING. BUT I WAS THERE.

ALL I WANT YOU TO KNOW IS THAT I DID SEE YOUR SONS AND YOUR DAUGHTERS IN THE UNIFORMS OF THE UNITED STATES OF AMERICA... FIGHTING FOR THE UNITED STATES OF AMERICA.

THIS BOOK, THIS REMEMBRANCE, IS DEDICATED TO THOSE WHO SO VALIANTLY SERVED IN WORLD WAR II - THE AMERICAN GIs AND MEN AND WOMEN OF THE ALLIED ARMED FORCES, NOTABLY, THOSE WHO SACRIFICED THEIR LIVES TO PROTECT OUR FREEDOM.

"There Won't Be War"

ALTHOUGH HITLER'S TYRANNY WAS NOT IGNORED, IT DID NOT APPEAR TO BE A THREAT TO THE UNITED STATES. AFTER ALL, IT WAS 1939 AND AMERICA WAS THOUSANDS OF MILES AWAY FROM ANY CONFLICT. FOR ME, THE YEAR WAS A GOOD ONE. I HAD A COUPLE OF FILMS PLAYING NATIONWIDE AND HAD COMPLETED A SUCCESSFUL FIRST YEAR ON RADIO FOR NBC.

AS A TREAT FOR HARD WORK, MY WIFE DOLORES AND I PLANNED A EUROPEAN HOLIDAY WITH A MAJOR STOP IN ENGLAND FOR A REUNION WITH MY FAMILY. (MY PARENTS WERE ENGLISH - WE WERE TOO POOR TO BE BRITISH.) AND AFTER ALL, I HAD LEFT WHEN I WAS FOUR. SURELY, ALL HAD BEEN FORGIVEN BY NOW.

WE SET SAIL ON THE NORMANDIE IN JULY WITH PLANS TO RETURN ON THE QUEEN MARY IN MID-SEPTEMBER.

AS WE BOARDED OUR SHIP A NEWSMAN ASKED IF WE "FEARED THE WAR CLOUDS HANGING OVER THE CONTINENT AND HITLER'S THREATS?" "THERE WON'T BE A WAR," I SAID WITH GREAT CONFIDENCE. (I'VE HAD TO EAT THOSE WORDS FOR 55 YEARS.)

WE HAD A GREAT TIME VISITING WITH MY RELATIVES OUTSIDE LONDON, THEN DOLORES AND I MADE OUR WAY TO PARIS. BUT OUR TRIP WAS CUT SHORT.

AMERICANS WERE BEGINNING TO SENSE WHAT SEEMED SO CLEAR TO INTERNATIONAL OBSERVERS: HITLER'S TROOPS WERE POISED TO MARCH. THE U.S. EMBASSY ISSUED A WARNING TO ALL U.S. CITIZENS ABROAD URGING THEM TO RETURN HOME. I SPENT THE NIGHT ON THE TRANSATLANTIC TELEPHONE WITH PARAMOUNT EXECUTIVES AND NBC RADIO BRASS WHO WANTED ME HOME AS SOON AS POSSIBLE.

RUMORS WERE FLYING THAT THE AUGUST 30 SAILING OF THE QUEEN MARY MIGHT BE THE LAST CIVILIAN CROSSING SO DOLORES AND I SCRAMBLED TO SOUTHAMPTON.

ON SEPTEMBER 3, HITLER INVADED POLAND. ENGLAND AND FRANCE DECLARED WAR ON GERMANY THE SAME DAY. EARLY ON THE MORNING OF SEPTEMBER 4, THE PASSENGERS GOT THE NEWS. DOLORES CAME BACK TO THE CABIN FROM MASS AND WOKE ME.

"YOU WERE WRONG," SHE SAID. "ENGLAND IS AT WAR."

"NOW, DOLORES..."

"BOB, YOU OUGHT TO SEE WHAT'S GOING ON UP IN THE SALON. PEOPLE ARE SOBBING. ONE WOMAN STOPPED ME AND SAID THERE

Dolores and I on the Queen Mary (1939), returning to the States. The forced smiles are not because of sea sickness, but because we were aware that German U-boats were watching us.

ARE GERMAN SUBMARINES WAITING FOR THE ORDER TO SINK THIS SHIP. THEY'VE ISSUED BLACKOUT INSTRUCTIONS AND PEOPLE ARE SCARED."

"THERE'S NOTHING TO BE FRIGHTENED ABOUT," I SAID. I DON'T THINK DOLORES BELIEVED ME. (IT MAY HAVE BEEN THE PITCH OF MY VOICE THAT GAVE ME AWAY.)

WE WERE SUPPOSED TO DO A SHIP'S CONCERT THAT NIGHT AND NOW I DIDN'T KNOW IF WE SHOULD. I WENT TO SEE THE CAPTAIN. HE WANTED THE SHOW TO GO ON. "COMEDY IS EXACTLY WHAT THE PASSENGERS NEED AT THIS TIME," HE SAID. SO I SPENT

THE REST OF THE AFTERNOON PUTTING TOGETHER A ROUTINE AND WRITING SPECIAL LYRICS TO *Thanks for the Memory*.

THAT NIGHT WAS THE CLOSEST I'D EVER COME TO HAVING STAGE FRIGHT. FORGET THE "STAGE" - LIKE EVERYONE ELSE, I WAS PLAIN FRIGHTENED. BUT AFTER A FEW MINUTES - THE PENDING TRAGEDY WAS FORGOTTEN FOR A LITTLE WHILE AND WE HAD SOME FUN. MY OPENING JOKE WAS: "THE STEWARD TOLD ME WHEN I GOT ON BOARD, 'IF ANYTHING HAPPENS IT'S WOMEN AND CHILDREN FIRST, BUT THE CAPTAIN SAID, IN YOUR CASE - YOU CAN HAVE YOUR CHOICE.'" I CLOSED THE SHOW WITH THE PARODY I HAD WRITTEN THAT AFTERNOON:

Thanks for the memory
Of this great ocean trip
On England's finest ship.
Tho' they packed them to the rafters
They never made a slip.
Ah! Thank you so much.

Thanks for the memory
Some folks slept on the floor,
Some in the corridor;
But I was more exclusive,
My room had "Gentlemen" above the door,
Ah! Thank you so much.

THAT CROSSING FELT LIKE IT TOOK AN ETERNITY. WHEN WE FINALLY DOCKED IN NEW YORK EVERYONE RECEIVED A WARM WELCOME FROM ANXIOUS RELATIVES. UNKNOWN TO US, THE QUEEN MARY'S SISTER SHIP, ATHENIA, HAD JUST BEEN SUNK BY THE GERMANS.

ONCE BACK HOME ON SOLID GROUND I BUSIED MYSELF WITH THE *The Road To Singapore* (THE FIRST "ROAD" MOVIE) WITH BING CROSBY AND DOROTHY LAMOUR. I FOLLOWED THIS WITH A SECOND FILM, *Ghostbreakers*, AND MY RADIO SHOW, WHICH WAS WELL ON ITS WAY TO BECOMING NUMBER ONE IN THE RATINGS. THE WAR IN EUROPE STILL SEEMED FAR AWAY; FAR ENOUGH FOR US TO TAKE SOME COMIC JABS AT "DER FUHRER."

FOR THOSE OF YOU WHO KNOW YOUR HISTORY - HITLER'S ARMIES HAD OVERRUN MOST OF WESTERN EUROPE AND THREATENED TO INVADE GREAT BRITAIN. OUR COUNTRY WENT TO GREAT MEASURES TO MAINTAIN AN OUTWARD SHOW OF NEUTRALITY, WHILE SUPPLYING BRITAIN WITH MUCH NEEDED WAR MATERIEL.

NEUTRAL OR NOT, THERE WAS A MILITARY BUILDUP AND THE LIFESTYLE FOR MOST AMERICANS WAS CHANGING. RECRUITING POSTERS STARTED SHOWING UP TOUTING SLOGANS LIKE - "JOIN THE ARMY - TRAVEL."

"This is Bob (Army Camp) Hope"

My LOVE FOR THE GI STARTED IN 1941 - MAY 6, TO BE EXACT. WE HAD JUST FINISHED A SCRIPT SESSION FOR MY RADIO SHOW WHEN I WAS APPROACHED BY MY PRODUCER AL CAPSTAFF IN THE PARKING LOT. HE ASKED, "HOW WOULD YOU LIKE TO DO A RADIO SHOW FOR THE MILITARY AT MARCH FIELD IN RIVERSIDE?"

"INVITE THEM TO THE STUDIO," I OFFERED.

"TOO MANY!" HE SAID.

"HOW MANY?" I ASKED.

"TWO THOUSAND."

I BLINKED - I COULD HEAR THE SOUND THAT 2,000 JOKE-HUNGRY SERVICEMEN COULD MAKE - ALL LAUGHING AND APPLAUDING. THIS WAS AN OFFER I COULDN'T RESIST.

WHAT AN AUDIENCE IT WAS. THE SHOW WAS PRODUCED IN OUR ESTABLISHED RADIO FORMAT WITH OPENING MONOLOGUE, CAST-MEMBER COMEDY, MUSIC, A GUEST STAR SKETCH AND THE USUAL COMMERCIALS. THE NEW DIFFERENCE WAS THE ADAPTATION OF OUR COMEDY TO A MILITARY CONTEXT:

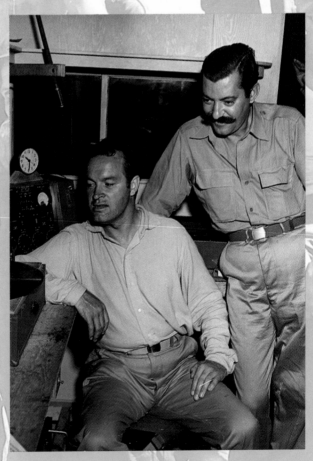

How do you do, ladies and gentlemen, this is Bob - March Field - Hope...telling all you soldiers that have to shoot in swamp or march in the brush, if they use Pepsodent no one will ever have to drill in your mush... Well, here we are at March Field, one of the Army's great flying fields, located near Riverside, California...and I want to tell you that I'm thrilled being here...and what a wonderful welcome you gave me...as soon as I got in the camp, I received a ten-gun salute...or so they told me on the operating table....These guys were glad to see me...one rookie came running up to me and said, "Are you really Bob Hope?" I said, "Yes!" ...they grabbed his rifle just in time...

Announcer Bill Goodwin, Elvia Allman ("Cobina") and yours truly took time out from our radio show to help the Red Cross blood bank. When I handed out my photos they wanted their blood back.

MY WRITERS HAD A BALL. THERE WAS HARDLY A SUBJECT WE WOULDN'T APPROACH. LAUGHS CAME FROM SIMPLE HAREBRAINED FOOLISHNESS, RELUCTANT HEROISM, AND EVEN BLATANT COWARDICE SET AGAINST A CLIMATE OF HIGH SERIOUSNESS. WE MADE A POINT OF RESEARCHING THE MILITARY LINGO AND COMMANDING OFFICERS' NAMES. THE STERN MILITARY REGIME EVOKED LAUGHS, SO DID THE SOLDIERS' RESENTMENTS, HARDSHIPS AND HABITS. THEY LAUGHED AT ME BUT MOST OF ALL, THEY LAUGHED AT THEMSELVES.

ON MAY 20, I TOOK GUEST STAR PRISCILLA LANE AND THE CAST TO THE SAN DIEGO NAVAL STATION. (SAILORS LIKE TO LAUGH, TOO.) AND THE FOLLOWING WEEK WE DID A SHOW FOR THE MARINES AT SAN LUIS OBISPO. AND ON JUNE 10, MARY MARTIN CAME WITH ME TO THE ARMY'S CAMP CALLAN. I WAS OFF AND RUNNING AND ENJOYING EVERY MINUTE SPENT ENTERTAINING THE MEN AND WOMEN IN UNIFORM.

Meanwhile, on the homefront - Jerry Colonna, who worked with youth groups between radio shows, tours and movies, gives an autograph to a member of the American Women's Volunteer Service (AWVS). Hey, that woman in uniform looks like Dolores. It is Dolores!

....

It was December 7, 1941, 11:20 a.m. I was in my car on the way to Lakeside Golf Course, listening to a football game from the Polo Grounds in New York. Suddenly, I heard words I couldn't believe. "The Japanese have bombed Pearl Harbor."

On Tuesday evening, December 9 - Pepsodent relinquished our airtime to President Roosevelt for his second declaration-of-war speech to the American people. The public and private reaction to the nation's crisis was sobering. That week, for the first time in my life, the opening monologue was a serious one:

Good evening, ladies and gentlemen... this is Bob Hope, and I just want to take a moment to say that last Tuesday night, at this time, I was sitting out there with you listening to our president as he asked all Americans to stand together in this emergency. We feel that in times like these - more than ever before, we need a moment of relaxation. All of us on the Pepsodent show will do our best to bring it to you. We think this is not a question of keeping up morale... to most Americans, morale is taken for granted. There is no need to tell a nation to keep smiling when it's never stopped. It's that ability to laugh that makes us the great people that we are... Americans! All of us in this studio feel that if we can bring into your homes a little of this laughter each Tuesday night, we are helping to do our part. Thank you...

....

1942 was a year of sacrifice in the United States. Moms and dads said goodbye to their children with a hug and a kiss, a tear and a silent prayer. Youngsters wondered where daddy was going and why. Wives parted from husbands, and courageous young men put their lives on hold, postponed their ambitions, and volunteered for the war effort because they knew "Uncle Sam needed them."

On the home front - not a man, woman or child was exempt from the war effort. Women flocked to the factories to take over jobs left vacant by men going to war; many of these jobs became assembly lines that made America's war machinery.

Across the country, school children were busy with paper drives, collecting

Anything for the war effort. You'd think I'd look happier with all these pretty gals around.

scrap metal, rubber tires, and tin foil, to help the war effort. Women saved cooking fat and turned it in to provide glycerine for the manufacture of gun powder and dynamite. They gave up their silk stockings for recycling

INTO PARACHUTES. VICTORY GARDENS BECAME AN IMPORTANT PASTIME FOR GROUPS AND INDIVIDUALS.

AMERICANS WERE ASKED TO MAKE DO WITH LESS. WARTIME RATIONING WAS A CONSEQUENCE OF THIS WAR. THE MILITARY HAD FIRST PRIORITY ON SUPPLIES. SIGNS OF THE TIMES WERE RATION BOOKS, RED MEAT TOKENS, AND A, B, C AND T GASOLINE STICKERS ON THE WINDSHIELDS OF CARS. THINGS TAKEN FOR GRANTED WERE NOW UNAVAILABLE - SUGAR, COFFEE, CHEWING GUM, CIGARETTES. COMPLAINTS? ...VERY FEW. SACRIFICE WAS PART OF EVERYONE'S PATRIOTIC CONTRIBUTION.

SACRIFICE, PRIDE AND HOPE WERE MORE THAN "BUZZ WORDS" OF THE PERIOD. THESE EMOTIONS WERE GENUINE AND WERE THE MORALE BUILDERS FOR ALL AMERICANS. IT WAS QUITE EVIDENT THAT THE STRENGTH OF THE NATION CAME FROM THE HEART AND SOUL OF ITS UNIFIED PEOPLE. IT WAS A UNIQUE AND SPECIAL TIME IN THE COUNTRY. WE HAD A COMMON GOAL AND WHAT WE WERE ABLE TO ACCOMPLISH WAS EXTRAORDINARY.

Soldiers in Greasepaint

HOLLYWOOD WENT TO WAR IN A BIG WAY. SOME OF ITS BIGGEST STARS ENLISTED - CLARK GABLE, JIMMY STEWART, GLENN MILLER, ROBERT CUMMINGS, DOUG FAIRBANKS JR., GLENN FORD, ALEC GUINNESS, VAN HEFLIN, CHARLTON HESTON, WILLIAM HOLDEN, LESLIE HOWARD, GENE KELLY, BURT LANCASTER, ROBERT MONTGOMERY, GENE AUTRY, PAUL NEWMAN, DAVID NIVEN, MICKEY ROONEY, ROBERT STACK, ROBERT WALKER AND ELI WALLACH, TO NAME A FEW. THOSE WHO WERE NOT IN THE ARMED FORCES, WERE GIVING THEIR TIME, TALENT AND RESOURCES ON THE HOME FRONT. IF THEY WERE NOT BUSY

The Hollywood Canteen was on a side street off Hollywood Boulevard. Movie stars pitched in, entertained, waited on tables, washed dishes and danced with the soldiers and sailors passing through. No officers were allowed and it got so crowded that if a soldier wanted to tune the radio, he'd have to squeeze past Lana Turner, Hedy Lamarr, Dorothy Lamour and Betty Grable to change a station. In five minutes I must have heard 148 different programs. Bette Davis was practically the den mother. Dinah Shore and I washed dishes with Vice President Henry Wallace, who wanted to show what a clean politician he was.

WITH BOND RALLIES, THEY WERE SERVING UP COFFEE AND CONVERSATION; SANDWICHES AND ENTERTAINMENT AT CANTEENS IN NEW YORK AND HOLLYWOOD. SOME MADE MOTIVATIONAL AND EDUCATIONAL FILMS, AND PUBLIC SERVICE ANNOUNCEMENTS; ROLLED BANDAGES, SERVED IN HOSPITALS AND WORKED WITH CIVIC GROUPS.

The Hollywood Victory Caravan was an idea of the U.S. Treasury Department - a trainload of fifty Hollywood names making whistle-stops across the country to sell war bonds. They had no trouble getting stars; who in Hollywood had the guts to tell the IRS he was going to be out of town?

ON APRIL 29, 1942, I TOOK FRANCES LANGFORD AND JERRY COLONNA TO WASHINGTON, D.C. WHERE WE CAUGHT UP WITH THE HOLLYWOOD VICTORY CARAVAN. THE CARAVAN WAS A SPECIAL TRAIN CARRYING SOME OF THE NATION'S MOST POPULAR ENTERTAINERS ACROSS THE COUNTRY, REHEARSING ON THE WAY, FOR THE KICKOFF OF A TWO-WEEK WHISTLE STOP TOUR FOR THE ARMY AND NAVY RELIEF FUNDS. CARAVAN STARS INCLUDED: DESI ARNAZ, JOAN BENNETT, JOAN BLONDELL, CHARLES BOYER, JAMES CAGNEY, CLAUDETTE COLBERT, BING CROSBY, OLIVIA DE HAVILLAND, CARY GRANT, CHARLOTTE GREENWOOD, BERT LAHR, LAUREL AND HARDY, GROUCHO MARX, FRANK MCHUGH, RAY MIDDLETON, MERLE OBERON, PAT O'BRIEN, ELEANOR POWELL, RISE STEVENS AND SPENCER TRACY - PLUS, OF COURSE, FRANCES AND JERRY.

THE SHOW WAS A THREE-HOUR VARIETY PACKAGE OF POPULAR SONGS, DANCES, COMEDY SKETCHES, DRAMATIC SCENES AND READINGS, EVEN OPERATIC ARIAS. CREATED BY PRODUCER-DIRECTOR MARK SANDRICH AND MUSICAL DIRECTOR ALFRED NEWMAN, THE SHOW WAS WRITTEN BY HEAVYWEIGHTS LINDSAY AND CROUSE, MOSS HART, GEORGE S. KAUFMAN AND JEROME CHODOROV WITH ORIGINAL MUSIC ADDED BY JEROME KERN, JOHNNY MERCER, FRANK LOESSER AND ARTHUR SCHWARTZ.

OUR LITTLE GROUP JOINED THE OTHERS AT A WHITE HOUSE LAWN PARTY GIVEN BY ELEANOR ROOSEVELT. THEN IT WAS OFF TO CONSTITUTION HALL FOR AN ALL-NIGHT REHEARSAL. BOSTON FOLLOWED WASHINGTON, THEN PHILADELPHIA, CLEVELAND, DETROIT, CHICAGO, ST. LOUIS, ST. PAUL, MINNEA-

Once on the train - the stars of the Hollywood Victory Caravan started rehearsals. Warming up - Cary Grant on the drums, Joan Blondell on the trumpet, Groucho Marx on the saxophone and Bert Lahr on the string bass. Of course, when the band returned to the car, after a five-minute break, all instruments had to be returned to their rightful owners.

The United States, the Axis - everybody had a propaganda machine going... so I thought I would try an organized scheme of my own. After all, WAC's should have pin-ups too.

POLIS, DES MOINES, HOUSTON AND DALLAS.

THE VICTORY CARAVAN WAS THE VANGUARD OF THE MOVIE INDUSTRY'S WAR EFFORT. THROUGH THE WAR ACTIVITIES COMMITTEE, HOLLYWOOD RAISED MILLIONS OF DOLLARS FOR THE USO, AND ARMY AND NAVY RELIEF SOCIETIES. IT SET AND KEPT A LONG-RANGE GOAL TO RAISE MORE THAN A BILLION DOLLARS IN WAR BONDS BY SENDING SEVEN TROUPES OF FILM STARS TO APPEARANCES IN 5,000 THEATERS LOCATED IN 300 CITIES ACROSS THE NATION.

HEY, WE WERE ON A ROLL. FOLLOWING THE VICTORY CARAVAN, FRANCES, JERRY AND I WERE OFF TO ENTERTAIN MORE GIS - 65 SHOWS AT A VARIETY OF MILITARY BASES AND HOSPITALS.

I SPENT THE SUMMER OF 1942 WORKING WITH SAM GOLDWYN: THAT IS, DURING THE WEEK I WORKED FOR GOLDWYN AND ON WEEKENDS I WORKED FOR ANOTHER SAM, DOING CAMP SHOWS AND PGA-ARRANGED WAR RELIEF GOLF BENEFITS WITH CROSBY.

ONE DAY MY FORMER STAND-IN, LYLE MORAIN, VISITED THE SET IN HIS SERGEANT'S UNIFORM. HE ASKED ME TO CONSIDER MAKING AN ENTERTAINMENT TOUR OF THOSE DESOLATE ALASKAN

I knew we had to work our way to entertain the troops - but jump-starting the plane was not what I had in mind. (That's Frances Langford laughing.)

BASES WHERE SOME OF HIS BUDDIES WERE STATIONED.

AL JOLSON HAD RECENTLY RETURNED FROM DOING SHOWS IN ALASKA, COMEDIAN JOE E. BROWN HAD TAKEN A LOAD OF ATHLETIC EQUIPMENT UP THERE AND EDGAR BERGEN TOLD ME THAT HE "RELISHED 13 SHOWS A DAY, DONE IN GUN EMPLACEMENTS, ON THE SIDES OF HILLS, THE BACKS OF TRUCKS, ON BARGES AND LANDING WHARVES." WELL, THAT SOUNDED GREAT FOR ME. (IT ALL REMINDED ME OF MY DAYS IN VAUDEVILLE.) SO I ASKED MY BROTHER JACK TO FIND OUT IF AN ALASKAN TOUR COULD BE ARRANGED.

A return visit to March Field, California with a radio show in 1942. Appears that the men there preferred me in the audience instead of on stage. From the smiles on their faces - Frances Langford was singing.

What a great way to help the war effort - golf, Bing and I sold a lot of war bonds playing the game.

SEPTEMBER FOUND FRANCES, JERRY AND OUR ONE MAN ORCHESTRA - GUITARIST TONY ROMANO, ALASKA-BOUND. WE LANDED IN FAIRBANKS AND WERE SOMEWHAT DISAPPOINTED TO SEE THAT THE AIRPORT LOOKED A LOT LIKE LOCKHEED IN BURBANK. WE WERE MET BY SPECIAL SERVICES CAPTAIN DON ALDER AND HIS PILOTS, CAPTAINS MARVIN SELTZER AND BOB GATES. THE PLANE WAS A STRIPPED-DOWN VERSION OF A DC-3 (KINDA LIKE A METAL LUNCH BOX WITH PROPELLERS). WE WERE TOLD TO ENJOY A FEW HOURS OF COMFORT BECAUSE EVERYTHING BEYOND FAIR-

Obviously, not everyone was pleased with my performance. This was taken following a radio show at Camp Roberts in February, 1942.

BANKS WAS RUGGED. (THAT BE-
CAME THE UNDERSTATEMENT OF
THE TRIP.)

THE NEXT MORNING WE HEADED
FOR NOME, WITH A STOP AT GALENA
FOR REFUELING. WHILE WE WAITED,
THE GIS SEEMED TO MATERIALIZE
FROM NOWHERE. WHEN THE CROWD
GATHERED, WE BROKE INTO OUR
ACT FROM THE BACK OF A TRUCK.
THE APPLAUSE WAS MUFFLED BY
HEAVY GLOVES, BUT THE LAUGHS
ECHOED OFF THE FROST OF THEIR
BREATH. FOR A HAM LIKE ME - IT
WAS WONDERFUL.

Oh, those GIs... they sure know how to make a person feel welcome.

WE HEADED FOR NOME AND
STARTED DOING SHOWS FOR SMALL
GROUPS IN QUONSET HUTS (THOSE ARE UPSIDE-DOWN FOX-
HOLES)...

This is our first trip up North and the Army has really taken care of us. They gave us a plane that was flown by a four-star general...Pershing...I knew it was an old plane when I saw the pilot sitting behind me wearing goggles and a scarf.

AS WE CAME OUT OF ONE HUT, THERE WERE 600 SOLDIERS
STANDING IN THE RAIN. IT WAS TOO COLD TO DO THE SHOW
OUTSIDE SO WE CRAMMED ALL 600 MEN INTO ANOTHER HUT...CA-
PACITY 300. FOR THE FIRST TIME, I REALLY KNEW WHAT IT WAS LIKE
TO PLAY TO A PACKED HOUSE. WE WERE WORKING ON THE STOVE.

ONE JOKE THAT EVERYBODY LOVED WAS ABOUT THE AIRMAN WHO WAS MAKING HIS FIRST PARACHUTE DROP. WELL, HIS FIRST LIEUTENANT TOLD HIM WHICH CORD TO PULL, AND TOLD HIM THAT WHEN HE HIT THE GROUND THERE WOULD BE A STATION WAGON WAITING TO DRIVE HIM BACK TO THE BASE. SO THE AIR-
MAN JUMPED OUT OF THE PLANE AND WHEN HE PULLED THE CORD
NOTHING HAPPENED, AND HE SAID, "AND I BET THE STATION
WAGON WON'T BE THERE EITHER."

Our shows in Alaska (1942) were performed in Quonset huts. It was close quarters but nobody minded - it was cold up there. All the show cast is in there someplace.

ON THE WAY TO ANCHORAGE FROM CORDOVA WE RAN INTO A LITTLE BAD WEATHER. I GUESS YOU CAN CALL HAIL AND SLEET (AND AT NIGHT) BAD WEATHER. THE CABIN STEWARD SAT DOWN NEXT TO FRANCES. HE REACHED UNDER HER SEAT AND TOOK OUT A PARACHUTE AND A MAE WEST. "YOU'D BETTER PUT THESE ON, WE MAY HAVE TO DITCH. IF WE HAVE TO ABANDON SHIP - PULL THIS. IF YOU SHOULD LAND IN WATER, PULL THIS ONE. BY THE WAY, I THINK WE'RE LOST."

"HOW BAD IS IT?" I ASKED.

"THEY'RE HAVING TROUBLE WITH THE RADIO."

JUST THEN THE PLANE FELT LIKE IT HAD BEEN SMACKED BY SOMETHING HARD. "WHAT WAS THAT?"

THE STEWARD ANSWERED, "FELT LIKE A PROP WASH FROM ANOTHER PLANE. MAN, THAT WAS CLOSE!"

"REMIND ME TO TELL YOU SOMETHING WHEN WE'VE ALL LANDED SAFE AND SOUND," LANGFORD SAID, SMILING.

"AND I BET THE STATION WAGON WON'T BE THERE EITHER," COLONNA SAID, EXPRESSIONLESS.

AFTER AN ETERNITY OF CIRCLING AND WAITING TO SEE IF ANYTHING WOULD CLEAR, WE SAW A JAB OF LIGHT AND THE PLANE DIPPED AND STARTED DOWNWARD. THE PLANE CAME OUT OF THE SOUP TO A BLAZE OF SEARCHLIGHTS. THE PROP WASH WE FELT WAS FROM A UNITED AIRLINES FERRY SERVICE PLANE THAT HAD RADIOED THE REPORT OF OUR BACKWASH. MAJOR GENERAL SIMON, COMMANDER OF THE ARMED FORCES IN ALASKA, ORDERED EVERY AVAILABLE SEARCHLIGHT TRAINED ON THE SKY. WHEN THE PILOTS SAW A FINGER OF LIGHT PIERCE THROUGH THE FOG, THEY TOOK A CHANCE THAT IT MIGHT BE THE FIELD.

I knew the living quarters would be small. But sharing them?

WHEN WE LANDED I ASKED FRANCES WHAT IT WAS SHE WANTED TO SAY NOW THAT WE WERE SAFE. "OH," SHE SAID, "I HAVE ALWAYS WANTED TO MAKE A PARACHUTE JUMP. I WAS REALLY HALF HOPING WE'D HAVE TO." ME? I NEEDED A CHANGE OF LAUNDRY.

THE NEXT DAY WE WERE IN SEATTLE DOING ANOTHER RADIO SHOW. AFTER WE FINISHED, WE LOOKED AT EACH OTHER AND SAID - LET'S GO BACK. AND WE DID.

WE FLEW BACK TO ANCHORAGE AND TO OUR FIRST STOP IN MAKNEK ON KICHAK BAY AND OUT TO UNIMAK ISLAND. THE TROOPS WERE SPREAD OUT ON COLD, WET GROUND. I SAW ONE KID SITTING ON HIS FEET AND ASKED "IF HE HAD TO WALK MUCH?" THERE WAS A SPRINKLE OF LAUGHTER AT THE QUESTION, BUT

THE BIG LAUGH CAME WHEN THE KID REPLIED, "I DON'T KNOW - BUT WHEN I ENLISTED I HAD FEET." THAT'S WHEN I REALIZED THAT WHAT THE GIs WANTED MOST, LIKED BEST AND NEEDED, WAS HUMOR TURNED ON THEMSELVES, A CHANCE TO VENT THEIR HARDSHIPS, THEIR FEAR, THEIR LONELINESS.

AT FORT GLEN, WHILE FRANCES WAS SINGING *You Made Me Love You*, TEARS STARTED STREAMING DOWN THE CHEEKS OF A YOUNG SOLDIER IN THE FRONT ROW. I SAW IT BUT PRETENDED NOT TO. ONE OF THE OFFICERS STANDING NEXT TO ME NUDGED MY ARM AND SAID, "GET THE KID." I FELT A SILLY TRICKLE RUNNING DOWN THE SIDE OF MY NOSE SO I TRIED NOT TO LOOK AT THE COMMANDING OFFICER, WHOM I COULD SEE OUT OF THE CORNER OF MY EYE WAS HOLDING BACK A TEAR. THEN WE LOOKED AT EACH OTHER AND - WELL, WE BOTH DAMN NEAR BAWLED.

MEANWHILE, BACK HOME IN THE MOVIES THEY PRODUCED, THE STUDIOS MADE A CONSCIOUS EFFORT TO ACKNOWLEDGE THE HEROISM AND SACRIFICE OF PEOPLE EVERYWHERE.

ON MARCH 4, 1943, AT THE ACADEMY AWARD CEREMONIES AT THE AMBASSADOR HOTEL'S COCONUT GROVE, PLASTER STATUETTES (REPLACED BY GOLD ONES AFTER THE WAR) WERE HANDED OUT TO GREER GARSON FOR HER COURAGEOUS *Mrs. Miniver* AND TO JIMMY CAGNEY FOR HIS ENERGETIC *Yankee Doodle Dandy*. BUT THE HIGHLIGHT OF THE EVENING WAS A MILITARY CEREMONY HEADED BY MARINE PRIVATE TYRONE POWER AND AIR CORPS PRIVATE ALAN LADD WHEN THEY UNFURLED A HUGE INDUSTRY FLAG THAT CARRIED THE NAMES OF 27,677 FILM WORKERS WHO WERE IN UNIFORM. SHOW BUSINESS WAS SERVING WELL ON THE WAR FRONT AND THE HOME FRONT.

The War Department created The Armed Forces Radio Service (AFRS). Every star in Hollywood contributed to one or more of the shows on AFRS, including - "Mail Call," "Jubilee" and "Command Performance." These programs were broadcast by short-wave or recorded on phonograph records, which the Air Force flew to fronts all over the world. Only once, on Christmas Eve, 1942, did "Command Performance" go public on all four American radio networks and all independent stations simulataneously - with some of the greatest entertainers in the world.

I Never Left Home

IN APRIL 1943, I ASKED MY BROTHER JACK TO WORK WITH THE UNITED SERVICES ORGANIZATION (USO), THROUGH ITS CAMP SHOW DIVISION, TO SEE HOW LONG A TOUR I COULD MAKE AND WHETHER OR NOT WE COULD BROADCAST THE RADIO SHOW FROM OVERSEAS. THE USO SAID, "O.K." PEPSODENT WAS ENTHUSIASTIC. I WAS HAPPY. DOLORES, GOD BLESS HER, ACCEPTED MY TRAVELLING WAYS.

WHEN I THINK BACK, I REALIZE HOW COURAGEOUS AND SELF-SACRIFICING DOLORES WAS. SHE ENCOURAGED ME TO DO WHAT I HAD TO DO. I THINK, TOO, OF ALL THE OTHER WIVES WHO WAITED FOR THEIR MEN AND KEPT THE HOME FIRES BURNING.

ONE OF MY MAJOR DISAPPOINTMENTS IN THE FINAL WEEKS OF PREPARATION FOR THE EUROPEAN USO TOUR WAS THAT CO-LONNA COULD NOT GO. HIS COMMITMENTS FOR FILM AND PER-SONAL APPEARANCES WERE BINDING. IN HIS PLACE I TOOK JACK PEPPER, A SONG-AND-DANCE MAN I'D KNOWN FROM VAUDEVILLE. FRANCES GOT RELUCTANT PERMISSION FROM HER ACTOR HUS-BAND JON HALL, AND TONY ROMANO WAS AVAILABLE.

IN LONDON WE WERE BOOKED AT CLARIDGE'S, AND WERE SURPRISED TO FIND THE HOTEL MANAGEMENT, DESPITE SHORT-AGES AND DEPLETED STAFF, REMAINED PROUD AND POISED. LONDONERS ACCEPTED BOMB DISFIGUREMENTS, TIGHT RATIONS AND A DAILY FEAR OF ATTACK WITH EXTRAORDINARY GOOD NATURE.

READY TO TRAVEL, WE BOARDED TWO 1938 HUDSONS AND A 1938 FORD PAINTED COUNTRYSIDE BROWN. OUR DRIVERS WERE FROM THE ENGLISH WOMEN'S CORPS - ZENA GROVES, EVE LUFF AND MARIE STE-WART. WE WERE OFF ON A REMARKABLE FIVE-WEEK ODYSSEY THROUGH THOUSANDS OF MILES OF UNMARKED LANES AND ROADS (INTEN-TIONALLY UNMARKED TO CONFUSE POTENTIAL INVADERS) ENTER-TAINING AT THREE AND SOMETIMES FOUR INSTALLATIONS A DAY.

I don't know where I am, but the audience was there; I was there. I joked; they laughed. And my pants and coat matched. (1943)

Anything for a girl in uniform. This girl is with England's Auxiliary Territorial Service (A.T.S. - the Women's Army). She wanted an autograph from a big name, so I signed Lawrence Olivier.

THE FIRST FULL SHOW WAS AT A BOMBER BASE CALLED EYE AERODROME. WE ARRIVED JUST BEFORE A MISSION WAS DUE TO FLY OUT. I STEPPED ON A MAKE-SHIFT STAGE WITH:

I've just arrived from the States. You know, that's where Churchill lives... he doesn't exactly live there... he just goes back to deliver Mrs. Roosevelt's laundry.

HEY, NOT VERY GOOD, I AD-MIT, BUT WE SOON DISCOVERED THAT YOU HAD TO BE PRETTY LOUSY TO FLOP IN FRONT OF THESE GUYS. THEY YELLED AND SCREAMED AND WHISTLED AT EVERYTHING.

WHAT WE CAUGHT FROM THE YELLS AND LAUGHS WAS THE SPIRIT OF THE MISSION. IT WAS CONTAGIOUS AND FROM THEN ON, THERE SEEMED TO BE NO LIMIT TO OUR ENERGIES. THE SECOND SHOW OF THE DAY WAS AT A FIGHTER BASE, THE THIRD AT A SUPPLY DEPOT AND THE FINAL SHOW WAS AT A LARGE HOSPITAL. ACTUALLY, WE DID A SERIES OF EIGHT TO TEN MIN-UTES IN A NUMBER OF DIFFERENT

We arrived in England to entertain the Allied Forces. They gave Frances a car with a driver... me, I got a bicycle with a tire patch kit.

WARDS. NO TIP-TOES FOR US - WE'D ENTER EACH WARD WITH MUSIC AND YELLS OF "DID YOU SEE OUR SHOW OR WERE YOU SICK BEFORE." OR SOMETHING LIKE, "ALL RIGHT, FELLAS, DON'T GET UP." THEY LAUGHED AND WE YELLED - TO COVER UP THE LUMPS THAT WERE CONSTANTLY GATHER-ING IN OUR THROATS. IT WAS HERE THAT WE CAME FACE-TO-FACE WITH THE GRIM REALITY OF WAR. HERE IS WHERE WE REALIZED WHAT WE WERE GIV-ING WAS SO INSIGNIFICANT COMPARED TO THE CONTRIBU-TION MADE BY THESE MEN.

Let me tell you, a man in a uniform will steal a laugh right out from under you. Here Col. C.A. Marion (left) and Capt. Billy B. Southworth give me some tips on how to play baseball in front of the 303rd Bomb Group stationed in England.

THE TROUPE MOVED WEST OF ENGLAND, TO WALES AND THEN BACK TO LONDON. SELFISHLY, THERE WERE TWO PEOPLE I WANTED TO SEE IN LONDON - THE KING AND WINSTON CHURCHILL. WELL, ONE OUT OF TWO IS NOT BAD. SENATOR HAPPY CHANDLER, FROM KENTUCKY, WAS IN LONDON AND ASKED ME TO ACCOMPANY HIM TO THE HOUSE OF COMMONS. I WAS PICKED UP AND A FEW MINUTES LATER THE CAR STOPPED IN FRONT OF 10 DOWNING STREET. HAPPY TOOK ME IN AND I STOOD WITH A GROUP OF SENATORS IN CHURCHILL'S STUDY. CHURCHILL

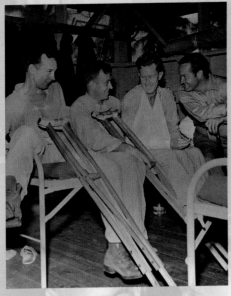

Hospital wards were the most difficult shows to do. They laughed when we yelled, "All right, fellas, don't get up." We yelled to cover up the lumps in our throats.

WALKED IN AND SUDDENLY I WAS IN A RECEIVING LINE, STANDING BEFORE CHURCHILL. THE PRIME MINISTER LOOKED - AND LOOKED AGAIN - AND SMILED. WE SHOOK HANDS AND I TOLD HIM WHAT A PLEASURE THIS WAS. BUT BEFORE WORDS COULD BE EXCHANGED, HE STEPPED OUT TO A SMALL GARDEN WITH THE SENATORS FOR A CONFERENCE. AMBASSADOR WINANT MOVED TO MY SIDE AND SUGGESTED I WAIT FOR SENATOR CHANDLER IN THE STUDY. I TOLD HIM I WASN'T GOING TO LEAVE UNTIL I GOT WINSTON CHURCHILL'S AUTOGRAPH ON A "SHORT SNORTER" (THAT'S AN ENGLISH FIVE-POUND NOTE THAT REPRESENTED A "PASS" FOR CROSSING THE ATLANTIC.) WHILE I WAITED FOR THE SIGNATURE, I TRIED ON ONE OF CHURCHILL'S HATS. WE WORE ABOUT THE SAME SIZE. WHAT A THRILL! AND

No one told me that the uniform of the day was dress whites.

NOW, I CONFESS TO ALL, A LITTLE LARCENY -- I POCKETED A PIECE OF HIS STATIONERY. WHAT GALL! (AND MY FATHER TOLD ME THAT I WOULD NEVER MAKE IT TO 10 DOWNING STREET.)

THE NEXT DAY WE WERE FLOWN TO PRESTWICK, SCOTLAND TO AWAIT TRANSFER TO NORTH AFRICA. WHILE WAITING FOR THE PLANE WE WERE ASKED TO PERFORM IN A STAGING AREA FOR NEWLY ARRIVED GIS FROM AMERICA. WE FINISHED THE SHOW WITH

A ROUSING CHORUS OF *We're Off on the Road to Morocco* - AND WE WERE! WE LANDED, LOOKED AROUND AND TOOK OFF FOR ALGIERS. THEN WHEN WE ARRIVED IN TUNIS, WE WERE WARMLY WELCOMED BY THE GREAT GENERAL JIMMY DOOLITTLE. WE IMMEDIATELY WENT TO WORK, FIRST, TWO SHOWS FOR THE RED CROSS, THEN FOR THREE DAYS WE ALTERNATED SHOWS BETWEEN BOMBER AND FIGHTER GROUPS:

Frances and I, with one of the greatest heros of World War II - General James "Jimmy" Doolittle. (He wasn't born - he was built by Boeing.) Happy to say that this meeting in Tunis, 1943, was the start of a long and beautiful friendship.

Hiya, fellow tourists... Well, I'm very happy to be here... but of course, I'm leaving as soon as I finish the show... but this is a great country... Africa... this is Texas with Arabs.

AND, AS SO FREQUENTLY HAPPENED, IT WAS A GI WHO PROVIDED THE BIG LAUGH AT THE SHOW. JUST AS I STEPPED UP TO THE MICROPHONE TO START THE SHOW, A LIGHT TANK CAME SHOVING THROUGH THE CROWD LIKE A FAT MAN MAKING FOR A SEAT IN A CROWDED SUBWAY CAR. PEOPLE GAVE WAY IN ALL DIRECTIONS. A TANK COMMANDS PLENTY OF RESPECT. I THOUGHT IT WAS OUT OF CONTROL. IT LOOKED AS IF THE THING WAS GOING TO MOW ME DOWN AND I WAS GETTING READY TO JUMP OFF THE PLATFORM WHEN SUDDENLY, RIGHT IN FRONT OF ME, IT STOPPED.

While touring in Africa, we met some more friends.

THE TOP FLEW OPEN AND A GUY CRAWLED OUT WEARING A TANKER'S CRASH HELMET AND GREASE ON HIS FACE. HE WAS DRAGGING A FOLDING CHAIR WHICH HE SET UP ON TOP OF THE TANK. HE SAT DOWN, CROSSED HIS LEGS, SMILED, WAVED AT ME, AND SAID, "MAKE ME LAUGH."

24

Home Was Never Like This

THE INVASION OF SICILY ON JULY 10, 1943 PAVED THE WAY FOR THE ARMY'S RELUCTANT DECISION TO LET OUR GROUP FLY TO PALERMO THREE DAYS LATER. IT WAS THE CLOSEST TO THE GROUND FIGHTING WE HAD BEEN OR WOULD GET; THE SMELL OF BATTLE WAS STILL IN THE AIR.

WE ARRIVED AT THE EXCELSIOR HOTEL IN PALERMO AFTER A DAY OF ENTERTAINING THE TROOPS. I WAS TIRED AND WENT TO BED AT ELEVEN-THIRTY. ALL OF A SUDDEN THERE WAS A DISTANT VOOM! AND I SAW A TRACER BULLET GO SCOOTING ACROSS THE SKY. WHEN I HEARD THE DRONE OF JU-88S (THAT'S A GERMAN JUNKER. IT THREW EVERYTHING AT YOU BUT HITLER'S SINK) I KNEW WE WERE IN FOR IT. THE DOCKS, WHICH WERE NATURALLY THE TARGET FOR THE RAID, WERE ONLY ABOUT TWO BLOCKS AWAY. THEY SAY WHEN YOU'RE DROWNING YOUR WHOLE LIFE FLASHES BEFORE YOUR EYES. I DON'T KNOW ABOUT YOU, BUT WITH ME IT'S THE SAME WAY WITH BOMBING. I THOUGHT OF MY FIRST PROFESSIONAL TOUR IN VAUDEVILLE...I THOUGHT OF ALL THE WONDERFUL THINGS I SHOULD HAVE SAID TO DOLORES AND MY KIDS...I THOUGHT OF EVERYTHING IN THE WORLD BUT GOING TO THE BOMB SHELTER IN THE BASEMENT. I BEGAN TALKING TO MYSELF AND WAS GETTING WEIRD ANSWERS. SUDDENLY, THE DIALOGUE WAS INTERRUPTED WHEN A BIG HUNK OF RED-HOT FLACK SAILED PAST MY WINDOW AND PLANES STARTED DIVE BOMBING. ONE NAZI, OBVIOUSLY AIMING FOR MY ROOM, ALSO LET GO WITH ALL HIS MACHINE GUNS ON THE WAY DOWN. AFTER YOU'VE LISTENED

Praise the Lord, and pass the ammunition; however, it looks as if we're aiming at the moon.

We're all gathered around the tail of a Nazi airplane to express our feelings. That fellow on the right is actor Bruce Cabot, serving as a Lieutenant in the U.S. Air Force.

TO A RAID FOR A LITTLE WHILE YOU BEGIN TO BE AFRAID THAT JUST THE NOISE WILL KILL YOU. THEN, AFTER YOU'VE LISTENED A LITTLE WHILE LONGER, YOU'RE AFRAID IT WON'T. YOU WANT TO CURL UP IN A BALL...YOU WANT THE BALL TO BE BATTED OUT OF THE PARK. YOU WANT A HOME RUN. OBVIOUSLY, WE SURVIVED, BUT IT IS AN EXPERIENCE I DON'T ENJOY RECALLING. AND I THINK OF THE BRAVE MEN WHO LIVED WITH THAT TERROR EVERY DAY AND STILL MANAGED TO DO THEIR JOBS.

THE NEXT DAY WE CROSSED SICILY TO DO SEVERAL SHOWS, INCLUDING ONE FOR THE 9TH DIVISION AND ANOTHER FOR THE

One of the greatest moments of my life was meeting General Dwight D. Eisenhower in Tunis (1943). This was before he became famous for his golf game and painting. Oh, as President of the United States, too.

1st Infantry, both between Palma and Licata. From Licata we were flown to Bone, Tunisia where we appeared for a big audience of soldiers, sailors, WACS, WRENS and Red Cross personnel in a staging area for more of the Italian invasion.

From Bone we flew to Kairouan (I don't make up these names - these places really do exist) to do two shows for the 82nd Airborne troops. We stayed overnight then headed for Algiers.

While in rehearsal for a broadcast from Algiers to the States I was informed that General Eisenhower would like us to come to his headquarters.

Meeting Dwight Eisenhower in the midst of that deadly muddle was like a breath of fresh air in a lethal chamber. It quieted us all, brought us all back to our senses and in every way paid us off for the whole trip.

Just before we departed Eisenhower gave us comforting words: "I understand you've had some excitement on your trip. Well, you're perfectly safe here and in Algiers. We haven't had a bombing in three months. We're too strong for 'em here. They can't get in." Please note, contrary to what we've all been told - generals can be wrong.

At about three in the morning, safely sound asleep in the Aletti Hotel, I was aroused by instructions to go to the bomb shelter. The next hour-and-a-half was one of the worst bombing raids Algiers had suffered. No one remained cool and unflapped after this raid.

I wanna tell ya - as the jargon goes - I was never so happy to be home.

The trip, the shows, the close calls had quite an effect on me. My priorities changed - I felt good about myself but realized that any contribution I was making was minimal. I was offering time and laughs - the men and women fighting the war were offering up their lives. Dedication to one's country took on a whole new meaning. I helped them laugh. They taught me what sacrifice was all about.

The Road To Normandy

FOR WEEKS AFTER RETURNING HOME FROM ALGIERS I HAD A GREAT TIME TALKING BY PHONE TO PARENTS, SWEETHEARTS AND CHILDREN OF GIs I MET ON THE TRIP. MY POCKETS WERE FULL OF LITTLE SLIPS OF PAPER WITH SCRAWLED NAMES, PHONE NUMBERS AND MESSAGES GIVEN TO ME TO BE DELIVERED. I WAS A LINK FROM THE WAR FRONT TO THE HOME FRONT. I LOVED EVERY MINUTE OF IT.

ONCE BACK HOME I BEGAN WORKING ON MY SIXTH SEASON WITH PEPSODENT - A SHOW EVERY WEEK FROM A DIFFERENT CAMP OR BASE WITH GUEST STARS LIKE MARLENE DIETRICH AND JIMMY DURANTE PLUS REGULARS FRANCES LANGFORD, JERRY CO-LONNA AND VERA VAGUE AND MY NEW BANDLEADER, STAN KENTON. SKINNAY ENNIS HAD JOINED THE ARMY. AND IN CASE YOU'RE WONDERING - LES BROWN WAS STILL WAITING IN THE WINGS.

The welcome home was always an important part of a trip. Here's Dolores, with Linda and Tony; and Flo Colonna with son, Robert, greeting Jerry and me when we returned from Africa.

On March 7th, I was in Florida for a radio show at an officers' training school with plans to be in Washington, DC on the 11th to emcee the Gridiron Dinner honoring President Roosevelt. I'd been waiting for an opportunity to do an in-person show for the President. I left Florida on the day of the event but weather conditions nearly cost me the chance to perform. I arrived late (an hour late, to be exact.) I had already been replaced by Ed Gardner (Duffy's Tavern) as emcee. Fritz Kreisler had played, Gracie Fields had sung and Elsie Janis had entertained, followed by a trained seal act (deja vu my vaudeville days.) Fred Waring and his Pennsylvanians were in full swing and I was to be the "tag end." I knew that after all that entertainment, including that damn trained seal - I had to be fresh. The head table was to my left. The audience had turned their chairs toward the small stage and were gauging their laughter by the reaction of the President. One thought kept running through my mind - I MAY BE IN TROUBLE!

Instead of my usual stroll onto the stage - I bounced into the spotlight. (I don't bounce too well, you know.)

Good evening, Mr. President, distinguished guests...I was late getting here because we flew through mud all the way...and then coming in from the airport I was on the bottom layer of the taxi...but I'm delighted to be here...I've always wanted to be invited to one of these dinners...and my invitation has been a long time in coming...I thought I had been vetoed by [Alben] Barkley [a Senator who was giving the President a hard time in Congress]...Perhaps I shouldn't mention Alben here...it's too much like talking about Frank Sinatra to Bing Crosby.

The first political jab at Roosevelt's problem with congress was a hit - so I pressed on. I referred to his (Roosevelt's) feud with the Chicago Tribune and that his dog Fala was the only dog ever house-trained on that newspaper. I pursued:

I think I should apologize to our President for some of the things I've said on radio. Especially about Mrs. Roosevelt. Like when Churchill and Roosevelt were discussing (war) campaign strategy, they talked about the enemy and how to keep Eleanor out of the crossfire.

I looked to my left. Roosevelt's head was tilted back and he was laughing, so was the audience. I was surprised that I was still standing.

On Tuesday, June 6, 1944, my broadcast season ended. Coincidentally, it was D-Day. With little or no time for prepared jokes or even ad libs, I went into session with my writers. I wanted to send a message to these dedicated warriors fighting for our freedom on the shores of Normandy:

You sat there and dawn began to sneak in, and you thought of the hundreds of thousands of kids you'd seen in camps the past two or three years...the kids who scream and whistle when they hear a gag and a song. And now you could see all of them again...in four thousand ships on the English Channel, tumbling out of thousands of planes over Normandy and the occupied Coast... in countless landing barges crashing the Nazi gate and going on through to do a job that's the job of all of us. The sun came up and you sat there looking at that huge black headline, that one great bright word with the exclamation point, "Invasion!" The one word that the whole world has waited for, that all of us have worked for. We knew we'd wake up one morning and have to meet it face to face, the word in which America has invested everything these thirty long months...the effort of millions of Americans building planes and weapons... the shipyards and the men who took the stuff across... little kids buying War Stamps, and working 'round the clock... millions of young men sweating it out in camps, and fighting the battles that paved the way for this morning. Now the investment must pay off - for this generation and all generations to come.

LIKE THE REST OF AMERICA AND THE FREE WORLD, I WAS LISTENING TO MY RADIO IN MY LIVING ROOM WAITING FOR ANY AND ALL NEWS OF THE INVASION. AND LIKE THE REST OF AMERICA I WAS THERE...ON THE BEACHES OF NORMANDY IN PRAYERS, IN SPIRIT AND HOPING THE TIDE AGAINST TYRANNY HAD TURNED. -THE TYRANNY IN EUROPE, AT LEAST. BUT THERE WAS STILL A MAJOR PART OF THE WAR TO BE FOUGHT - IN EUROPE AND MOST CRUCIALLY, IN THE PACIFIC WHERE OUR ARMED FORCES WERE READYING MASSIVE FORCES FOR VICTORY AT SEA - VICTORY OVER JAPAN.

....

AFTER THE ATTACK ON PEARL HARBOR, AMERICANS HEADED FOR A WORLD GLOBE OR ATLAS TO FIND PLACES NOW TALKED ABOUT IN THE DAILY NEWSPAPERS AND ON THE RADIO. PLACES I COULDN'T SPELL. HELL, PLACES I HAD NEVER EVEN HEARD ABOUT.

THE FIRST DAYS OF THE WAR IN THE PACIFIC WERE DISASTROUS. JAPAN QUICKLY CAPTURED THE PHILIPPINES, MALAYA, BURMA, INDONESIA AND MANY PACIFIC ISLANDS. BY MID-1942 THE JAPANESE HAD ADVANCED AS FAR AS THE ALEUTIAN ISLANDS AND NEW GUINEA. HOWEVER, THERE WAS ONE BRIGHT SPOT IN THE SPRING OF 1942. OUT OF THE BLUE, A FORMATION OF U.S. AIR FORCE PLANES UNDER THE COMMAND OF COLONEL JIMMY DOOLITTLE, FIRE-BOMBED THE CENTER OF TOKYO. THESE 'DOOLITTLE RAIDERS' FLEW MODIFIED B-25 BOMBERS FROM THE AIRCRAFT CARRIER USS HORNET. THEY DROPPED THEIR BOMBS AND HEADED FOR CHINA.

AUSTRALIA BECAME THE BASE FOR THE ALLIED FORCES (THE UNITED STATES, BRITAIN AND THE NETHERLANDS) FOR THE COUNTERMOVE AGAINST JAPAN. THE COMMAND WAS DIRECTED BY GENERAL DOUGLAS MACARTHUR, ADMIRAL CHESTER W. NIMITZ AND ADMIRAL WILLIAM F. HALSEY. (IN CASE YOU THOUGHT I'D FORGOTTEN - GENERAL GEORGE C. MARSHALL WAS SERVING AS ARMY CHIEF OF STAFF IN WASHINGTON, D.C.)

THE FIRST ALLIED SUCCESSES WERE SCORED IN THE BATTLES OF THE CORAL SEA AND ON MIDWAY. ON LAND THE ALLIED FORCES TOOK THE OFFENSIVE ON NEW GUINEA AND LANDED ON GUADALCANAL IN THE SOLOMON ISLANDS IN AUGUST 1942. VICIOUS BATTLES AT SEA AND ON BEACHHEADS FORCED THE ENEMY OUT OF THEIR STRONGHOLDS. THE PRICE OF THESE ONE-BY-ONE VICTORIES WAS TOO HIGH - THEY WERE PAID FOR WITH THE LIVES OF OUR VALIANT SAILORS, MARINES, AND SOLDIERS: OUR NATION'S PRIDE.

IN LATE 1943, AFTER SUCCESSFUL CAMPAIGNS IN THE SOLOMON ISLANDS AND NEW GUINEA (1944), THE ALLIED FORCES CONVERGED ON JAPAN THROUGH SCATTERED ISLAND GROUPS - THE PHILIPPINES, THE MARIANAS, IWO JIMA AND OKINAWA. WITH MOST OF ITS NAVAL UNITS SUNK, JAPAN BEGAN TO STAGGER.

The Pineapple Circuit

IN THE SUMMER OF 1944 I COULD HARDLY WAIT TO FINISH THE PRINCESS AND THE PIRATE FOR GOLDWYN STUDIOS SO THAT I COULD TAKE A USO TOUR TO THE SOUTH PACIFIC WAR ZONES.

ONE MORE TIME I SAID GOOD BYE TO DOLORES, LINDA AND TONY. I ASKED A PRETTY YOUNG DANCER, PATTY THOMAS, AND AN OLD VAUDEVILLE PAL, BARNEY DEAN, TO JOIN ME AND THE HOPE GYPSIES -

All dressed up and a lot of places to go. The Hope Gypsies - Frances Langford, Tony Romano, Jerry Colonna, Barney Dean and Patty Thomas arrive in Hawaii to 'work' the Pineapple Circuit.

"Mother" Langford, "Stash" Colonna, and "The Band" Romano for the tour. The military had provided us with a plane, a somewhat battered C-54 headed for Saipan to pick up some wounded. The plane didn't inspire our confidence but it did get off the ground.

Our first stop was Honolulu, which was 'Grand Central Station' for the Pacific area. On July 12, 1944 we gave our first show for the servicemen and women in Maluhia. For the next three days we toured the hospital wards at the Alieu Naval Hospital and Tripler Hospital. We followed with shows in the Nimitz Bowl, at the Jungle Training Center, Fort Hase and one for the civilian workers at the Navy Yard. It was on Kauai we were told that we were going to play the Pineapple Circuit where we were to perform for the greatest audience anyone could ask for.

The gang and I loved performing in front of the large crowds, but it was meeting with the soldiers in the hospitals that really touched our hearts.

We headed south for Christmas Island, a piece of rock 1500 miles away, where we played baseball and gave a show for 650 GIs and over a million blister bugs and land crabs. We crossed the equator to Canton Island whose flora consisted of one palm tree that the men stationed there affectionately called "the Coconut Grove" after the popular L.A. night club.

TARAWA WAS THE NEXT STOP ON OUR SCHEDULE BEFORE OUR FLIGHT TO ENIWETOK. AT THE SHOW THERE I REMARKED TO THE AUDIENCE,

"What an island. When the tide comes in, you guys should get submarine pay. You're not defending this place, are you? Let them take it, it'll serve them right."

If I were in Pasadena, I could be my own Rose Parade float.

THEY LAUGHED AT THE JOKES BUT YOU CAN IMAGINE WHAT HAPPENED WHEN I BROUGHT FRANCES AND PATTY ON STAGE. THE WOLF WHISTLES BLEW THREE PLANES OFF THE RUNWAY. IT FELT GOOD TO BRING GIRLS AND MUSIC AND LAUGHS TO PLACES WHERE BEFORE, THE ONLY THING BREAKING THE MONOTONY WAS FINDING A NEW FUNGUS GROWING ON YOU. EVERY TIME I STARTED TO GET A SWELLED HEAD FROM ALL THE APPLAUSE, BARNEY DEAN REMINDED ME THAT IT DOESN'T TAKE MUCH TO BE MORE POPULAR THAN JUNGLE ROT.

OFF ENIWETOK, WE WERE INVITED ABOARD A NAVY SHIP TO HAVE DINNER WITH ADMIRAL

Entertaining the troops during WWII wasn't easy, but someone had to do it.

HOOVER. I UNEXPECTEDLY RAN INTO HENRY FONDA. I WAS SO HAPPY TO MEET SOMEBODY FROM LaLa LAND THAT WE ALMOST KISSED RIGHT THERE ON THE DECK. HANK WAS IN THE NAVY, QUARTERED THREE DECKS BELOW. WITH A LOT OF COAXING, HANK ACCEPTED THE ADMIRAL'S INVITATION TO HAVE DINNER WITH US.

Were we happy to see someone from LaLa Land. Henry Fonda was not with a USO show but serving his country as an officer in the US Navy.

Photo right: Dolores forgot to pack my razor.

The Mosquito Network
or N.B.C. with D.D.T.

A LITTLE LESS THAN MIDWAY THROUGH OUR TRIP WE WERE ON KWAJALEIN - A BEAUTIFUL PLACE FROM THIRTY-THOUSAND FEET UP.

According to Colonna, "It looked like a diamond in the rough. But when we get down to the rough, it looks like somebody swiped the diamond."

IN ADDITION TO THE STAGE SHOW THERE, WE DID A SHOW FOR THE ARMED FORCES RADIO NETWORK MOST COMMONLY CALLED THE "MOSQUITO NETWORK." THE STATION COVERED A LARGE PORTION OF THE MID-PACIFIC AREA. IT WAS HEARD AS FAR AWAY AS SAIPAN ON ONE SIDE AND GUADALCANAL ON THE OTHER. BROADCASTS OF G.I. JOURNAL, MAIL CALL AND COMMAND PERFORMANCE WERE RELAYED FROM KWAJALEIN, EITHER BY

"Dr." Colonna and I did a broadcast on the network with a sting.

SHORT WAVE FROM THE UNITED STATES, OR BY TRANSCRIPTION. ALL WITHOUT COMMERCIALS, OF COURSE.

ON OUR WAY TO MAKIN WE PASSED OVER MILI ATOLL - PART OF THE MARSHALLS STILL HELD BY THE JAPANESE. WE HEARD ANTI-AIRCRAFT GUNS EXPLODING BELOW BUT WE DIDN'T SEE ANY FLAK. IN FACT, IT WAS IMPOSSIBLE TO SEE ANYTHING...WE ALL HAD OUR EYES CLOSED...PRAYING. NEEDLESS TO SAY, WE WERE HAPPY TO LAND. AND EVEN HAPPIER WHEN AT LUNCH, WE WERE SERVED SOMETHING WE HADN'T SEEN IN A LONG TIME - STEAK! AND NOT ONLY STEAK BUT FRESH MILK AND FRESH VEGETABLES, MASHED POTATOES, CRANBERRY SAUCE, FRENCH PASTRY AND ICE CREAM. FRANCES TOOK A LOOK AT THE DISPLAY OF FOOD AND SAID,

I guess he's already heard that joke.

A rare commodity on the South Pacific road was good food. On Makin Island the food looked so good that no one thought of their figures. In fact, it looked so good that no one thought of Patty's figure.

37

"Remove the mirage and bring on the food." Patty exclaimed, "It looks so good that I'm not going to think of my figure." To which I had to reply, "The food looks so good, that I'm not going to think of your figure either."

A NATIVE DELEGATION MET US WHEN WE LANDED ON MAJURO ISLAND AND IT WAS THAT SAME NATIVE POPULATION WHO ATTENDED OUR SHOW. I DID MY USUAL MONOLOGUE - TEN MINUTES OF JOKES AND FOR THAT TEN MINUTES THERE WAS A DEAFENING SILENCE. THEY JUST DIDN'T SEEM TO GET IT. THEN PATTY CAME OUT AND DID HER DANCE AND FRANCES SANG HER SONG. THIS, THEY UNDERSTOOD.

Critics everywhere! The natives of Bougainville must have heard about my act from Vasco Nunez de Balboa.

The Road To Pavuvu!

*A*FTER MAJURO, WE MADE OUR FIRST TRIP TO GUADALCANAL WHERE WE TOOK AN ARMY CATALINA FLYING BOAT (A PATROL BOMBER WITH DUCK INSTINCTS) AND ISLAND HOPPED ALL OVER THE PACIFIC - EMIRAU, GREEN ISLAND, TWO DAYS OF SHOWS AT BOUGAINVILLE, ON TO TREASURY AND TO THE RUSSELL ISLAND GROUP. THE ISLANDS WERE GETTING SMALLER AND SMALLER AND THE BASES GETTING MORE AND MORE PRIMITIVE. THE LAUGHS CAME WITH LINES LIKE,

"What a beautiful swamp you have here... This'd be a good spot to build a cesspool...If you wanna hide from your draft board, this is the place to do it."

WE DID SHOWS FROM PLACES THAT WEREN'T EVEN ON A MAP. ONE SUCH PLACE WAS A TINY ISLAND CALLED PAVUVU. WE WERE AT AN ISLAND BASE NAMED MBANIKA WHEN THE COMMANDER TOLD US THAT THE MEN OF THE FAMOUS 1ST MARINE DIVISION HAD BEEN TRAINING AT PAVUVU FOR ALMOST SIX MONTHS. THEY WERE PREPARING TO INVADE ANOTHER UNKNOWN ISLAND CALLED PELELIU, A TINY DOT IN THE CAROLINES, NORTH OF NEW GUINEA. PELELIU WAS RUMORED TO BE ONE OF THE MOST DANGEROUS JAPANESE-HELD POSITIONS ON THE WAY TO TOKYO. IN ALL THESE SIX MONTHS, THE MARINES HAD NO ENTERTAINMENT. HELL, THEY DIDN'T EVEN HAVE AN AIRSTRIP. WE'D HAVE TO LAND ON ROADS.

WE CLIMBED INTO PIPER CUBS, JUST ONE OF US AND A PILOT TO EACH TINY PLANE, AND FLEW OUT OVER THE PACIFIC. WHEN WE FINALLY LOCATED PAVUVU, WE BUZZED THE BASEBALL FIELD AND IT WAS THE MOST EXCITING MOMENT OF THE TOUR WHEN WE SAW FIFTEEN THOUSAND MEN WAITING FOR US, LOOKING UP AND CHEERING EACH LITTLE PLANE AS IT CAME IN. WE GAVE THE BEST SHOW OF THE TOUR.

WHEN THE MARINES FINALLY MADE THEIR ASSAULT ON PELELIU THEY FOUND THE CORAL REEFS STEEP AND JAGGED, THE TEMPERATURE 115 DEGREES, AND THE JAPANESE ENTRENCHED IN CAVES THEY HAD TURNED INTO FORTRESSES OF REINFORCED CONCRETE. OF THE FIFTEEN THOUSAND KIDS WHO CHEERED THAT DAY, 40 PERCENT NEVER WENT HOME. SOME MONTHS LATER I WAS GOING THROUGH A MILITARY HOSPITAL IN OAKLAND, CALIFORNIA, DOING THE USUAL "DON'T GET UP" ROUTINE FOR A WARD FULL OF WOUNDED MARINES WHEN A GUY, HALF-COVERED WITH

Patty and Frances were smiling... until they found out that this Piper Cub was their transportation to Pavuvu.

BANDAGES, SUDDENLY STUCK HIS HAND OUT OF THE BED COVERS AND HOLLERED AT ME, "PAVUVU." HE DIDN'T HAVE TO SAY ANYTHING ELSE. I JUST WENT OVER AND SHOOK HIS HAND, TURNED AND WALKED AWAY. I JUST COULDN'T HANDLE IT.

A small but "choice" audience. We got to exchange a few laughs with some wounded GIs being evacuated from Saipan, during our tour through New Caledonia.

FROM PAVUVU WE RETURNED TO GUADALCANAL FOR TWO MORE DAYS OF SHOWS - OUR LARGEST AUDIENCES OF THE TRIP - 86,000 SERVICEMEN, INCLUDING THE NATIVES. AT MOST OF OUR VENUES, THE NATIVES WOULD ATTEND THE TROOP SHOWS BUT THEIR SENSE OF HUMOR WAS SLIGHTLY DIFFERENT THAN OURS - THEY ALWAYS LAUGHED IN THE WRONG PLACES. HEY, THIS WAS THE IDEAL AUDIENCE. THE SOLDIERS LAUGHED AT THE

With our jokes, we needed a little protection.

JOKES AND THE NATIVES FELL OUT OF THEIR SEATS AT THE STRAIGHT LINES. THAT'S WHAT WE CALLED IN VAUDEVILLE - EGG-PROOF!

ON AUGUST 9 WE HIT TULAGI, MOVED TO THE NEW HEBRIDES AND ESPIRITU SANTO ISLAND (CODE NAME "BUTTONS"). THEN ON TO NEW CALEDONIA WITH A DESTINATION OF SYDNEY, AUSTRALIA FOR SOME WELL EARNED REST. HOWEVER....

S.O.S. - The Real Thing!!!

THE PROSPECT OF CLEAN LAUNDRY AND SLEEP MADE THE ALL-DAY FLIGHT ON OUR CATALINA FLYING BOAT BEARABLE AND THE WHOLE CREW WAS IN GOOD SPIRITS. OUR PILOT WAS LT. FRANK FERGUSON WHO SUCCUMBED TO MY

NAGGING TO LET ME TAKE OVER THE CONTROLS OF OUR PBY. ALL OF A SUDDEN, ALL HELL BROKE LOOSE -THE LEFT MOTOR CONKED OUT AND THE PLANE STARTED TO DIP. FERGUSON ORDERED ME OUT OF THE SEAT, STARTED CHECKING INSTRUMENTS AND AFTER FEATHERING THE PROP, YELLED, "JETTISON EVERYTHING WE DON'T NEED!" I RACED BACK TO THE CABIN AND TOLD EVERYBODY WE WERE IN SERIOUS TROUBLE AND TO JETTISON EVERYTHING THAT WAS LOOSE. WE BEGAN TOSSING OUT LUGGAGE, SOUVENIRS, CASES OF SCOTCH - ANYTHING THAT WASN'T FASTENED DOWN. BARNEY GOT INDIGNANT WHEN WE STARTED EYEING HIM.

WE WERE NEAR THE LITTLE TOWN OF LAURIETON WHEN THE PILOT SPOTTED A SMALL LAKE AND ON ONE COMPLAINING ENGINE BROUGHT US DOWN. THE PLANE SKIPPED TWICE, HIT A SANDBAR AND LURCHED TO A STOP. WE CRAWLED OUT ON A WING AND SHOUTED WITH RELIEF WHEN WE SAW A SMALL BOAT HEADED OUR WAY JUST AS WE STARTED TO SINK. WHEN THE AUSSIE SAW US CLINGING TO THE WING, HE HOLLERED, "I SAY, DO YOU CHAPS HAVE ANY AMERICAN CIGARETTES?" WE TRAVELED NINE THOU- SAND MILES FOR A LUCKY STRIKE COMMERCIAL.

HE TOOK US ASHORE. WE LOCATED SEVERAL VEHICLES AND DRIVERS TO TAKE US TO LAURIETON WHERE WE WERE GREETED BY THE TOWNSPEOPLE AND WERE ASKED TO DO A SHOW. THEY HAD A SMALL STAGE AND WE PERFORMED FOR THE ENTIRE POPULATION OF THE TOWN - AN AUDIENCE OF ABOUT FIVE

We made a hair-raising landing in Laurieton, and the first thing the Aussie asked us was if we had any American cigarettes... so I showed him we did.

Our stages came in many shapes and sizes... but on the fo'c's'le of a PT boat was pushing it just a litte.

HUNDRED INCLUDING DOGS, CATS AND A KANGAROO OR TWO.
THEY WERE SO HAPPY TO HAVE VISITORS THAT THEY NEVER SENT
OUT WORD THAT WE WERE SAFE. FOR THREE DAYS DOLORES
HEARD REPORTS THAT OUR PLANE WAS MISSING. I LATER LEARNED
THAT HAD OUR PLANE HIT THE SANDBAR FIRST, IT WOULD HAVE
EXPLODED.

WE FINALLY GOT TO SYDNEY VIA NEWCASTLE FOR A LITTLE
R&R AND THEN BACK TO THE JUNGLES FOR ANOTHER ROUND
OF ISLAND HOPPING...STARTING WITH NEW GUINEA; FIRST STOP,
HOLLANDIA THEN NOEMFOOR, WHERE THE BLACK WIDOW NIGHT
FIGHTERS WERE BASED. WE HAD JUST COMPLETED A SHOW THERE
WHEN WE GOT WORD THAT AN ENEMY SOLDIER HAD BEEN KILLED
TWO HUNDRED YARDS FROM THE STAGE DURING THE SHOW. I
HAD TO ASK, "WAS HE COMING OR GOING?"

WE CONTINUED ON TO WAKDE, OWI, AITAPE, (CAN YOU BELIEVE
THESE NAMES) AND TOOK PT BOATS TO DO SHOWS ON THE
ISLANDS OF WOENDI (REFERRED TO AS "WENDY" BY THE NAVY,)
ENDILA, LUMBRUM, LOS NEGROS, MANUS, PONAM AND PITYLU.

SIDEBAR: 18 YEARS LATER, IN THE ROSE GARDEN AT THE
WHITE HOUSE, PRESIDENT KENNEDY PRESENTED ME WITH THE
CONGRESSIONAL GOLD MEDAL. LATER HE TOLD ME HE WAS ONE
OF THOSE GUYS WHO SAT IN THE RAIN ON WENDY ISLAND AND
WATCHED OUR SHOW.

A young John F. Kennedy was in the audience at our rain-drenched show on Wendy Island.
Eighteen years later President Kennedy gave me the Congressional Gold Medal... I guess he liked
our act.

On August 31st, after some 30,000 miles, nearly 100 shows in 51 days to an audience of 545,751 (American GIs and nurses, members of the Allied Forces, and islanders plus one enemy soldier) we headed for home. And what a homecoming it was. We were met with open arms by our loved ones. Coming home is the most welcomed part of going to war...Just ask any GI.

Patty looks on as Frances gets ready for a pedicure on Hollandia. Lots of luck.

Pinning a red cross button on Truman.

Meanwhile, Back Home

BACK IN THE STATES WE CAUGHT UP ON WHAT HAD BEEN GOING ON DURING THE SUMMER IN EUROPE. WE HAD ALMOST FORGOTTEN ABOUT THAT FRONT WHILE WE WERE LEARNING TO PRONOUNCE "KAOPECTATE" IN FOUR NATIVE LANGUAGES.

WE LEARNED ABOUT THE FAILED ASSASSINATION ATTEMPT ON ADOLF HITLER BY SOME OF HIS OWN GENERALS, THE LIBERATION OF PARIS AND THE ALLIED TROOPS HAD CROSSED THE GERMAN BORDER. IN FACT, THE FEELING OF VICTORY WAS IN THE AIR AS WE DID THE FIRST PEPSODENT SHOW OF THE FALL SEASON AT THE MARINE CORPS AIR STATION IN THE MOJAVE DESERT.

AND A LOT OF THINGS WERE HAPPENING ON THE HOLLYWOOD FRONT. VINCENTE MINNELLI HAD DIRECTED A FILM CALLED MEET ME IN ST. LOUIS STARRING HIS WIFE, JUDY GARLAND; CROSBY GAVE HIS OSCAR WINNING PERFORMANCE IN GOING MY WAY; AND PARAMOUNT RELEASED OUR ROAD TO UTOPIA WHERE I FINALLY GOT LAMOUR.

NATIONALLY, THE PRESIDENTIAL CAMPAIGN WAS A HEATED ONE. FRANKLIN D. ROOSEVELT WAS RUNNING FOR AN UNPRECE-DENTED FOURTH TERM WITH HARRY S. TRUMAN AS HIS RUNNING MATE. THEIR OPPONENT WAS NEW YORK GOVERNOR THOMAS E. DEWEY. "CHARISMA" IS ONE OF THE MOST OVERWORKED WORDS IN THE ENGLISH LANGUAGE. I'M NOT SURE WHAT IT MEANS BUT I KNOW THAT ROOSEVELT HAD IT. MAYBE CHURCHILL SAID IT BEST: "MEETING FRANKLIN IS LIKE OPENING A BOTTLE OF CHAM-PAGNE."

NOVEMBER 7, 1944, WAS A TUESDAY, BUT THE PEPSODENT SHOW DIDN'T AIR - SOME FOOLISH LISTENERS PREFERRED TO HEAR THE ELECTION RESULTS. FDR WON BY A LANDSLIDE. EVEN SO, IT WAS A TOUGH POLITICAL BATTLE AND THE STRAIN WAS BEGINNING TO SHOW.

WHEN 1945 DAWNED, HISTORY WAS MOVING SO FAST THAT WE HARDLY HAD TIME TO WRITE MONOLOGUES ABOUT IT. THE WAR IN EUROPE HAD BECOME A RACE TO BERLIN BEFORE THE RUSSIANS GOT THERE AND DRANK UP ALL THE BEER.

THEN CAME OUR BROADCAST OF APRIL 17.

"This is Bob Hope, ladies and gentlemen. A few seconds ago we listened to the voice of Harry S. Truman, thirty-third president of the United States of America. No man on earth today, or all the way back through history, has faced so great a responsibility as President Truman. One hundred and thirty million Americans are serving notice that they will stand beside him to the completion of the task to which Franklin Roosevelt gave his life."

During the tour of England in 1943 we played to British and American servicemen and women at Royal Albert Hall. We were all on key but I was out of step.

THE WHOLE NATION MOURNED THE DEATH OF ONE OF THE WORLD'S GREATEST LEADERS. AND IF WE WERE NERVOUS ABOUT A MISSOURI HABERDASHER TAKING OVER THE REINS OF THE COUNTRY, HE SOON WON OUR CONFIDENCE. HE PUT A NOW FAMOUS SIGN ON HIS DESK IN THE OVAL OFFICE, *The Buck Stops Here*. OF COURSE A BUCK IN THOSE DAYS WAS STILL WORTH A DOLLAR.

EVERYTHING WAS HAPPENING AT ONCE IN THE WAR. THE ITALIANS CAPTURED MUSSOLINI AND HUNG HIS MISTRESS UPSIDE DOWN BESIDE HIM. THE RUSSIANS CAPTURED THE REICHSTAG IN BERLIN, AND HITLER TURNED A GUN ON HIMSELF.

On The Road To Peace

On May 8, 1945 we were entertaining the servicemen and women at the U.S. Naval Training Center in Oceanside, California, when we got the news about the victory in Europe. What a celebration we had! America took a couple of days to recover but then it was back to the task of winning the war in the South Pacific.

The U.S. soldiers in Germany didn't know if they were going to be shipped to the States or the meat grinder in the Pacific. The government decided they should have a little entertainment in the meantime.

I rounded up some new talent - singers Gale Robbins and Ruth Denas (who also pumped a mean accordion) and comedian Jack Pepper who joined regulars Jerry Colonna and Patty Thomas. We left on the Queen Mary. This time, we were informed that there was no danger. However, I kept seeing periscopes in front of my eyes until I realized it was my nose.

We did our first show at Albert Hall in London on the 4th of July in front of ten thousand GIs. After the first laugh, I stopped being nervous. More than ever now, our group represented home to them. I guess a lot of the laughter was homesickness, but like I said, "I'll take 'em any way I can get 'em."

From London we went to the USO Headquarters in Chatou, near Paris, where I felt like we had walked into central casting for Broadway and Hollywood. I ran into Alfred Lunt and Lynn Fontanne, Bea Lillie, Reginald Gardiner. It was great to see Cagney, Cooper, Ann Sheridan and Paulette Goddard. We were told we had just missed Jack Benny, Larry Adler, Ingrid Bergman, Al Jolson, Fred Astaire and Crosby. All of them made offshore trips for GIs and never said a word about it. So different from YOU-KNOW-WHO...

We joked, sang and danced our way across France - Amiens, Marseille (lots of army nurses in Marseille), Nice, Cannes and Germany.

On August 6, as we were preparing for a show in Bremerhaven for the Army's 29th Division, the world entered a new age. The atomic bomb was dropped on Hiroshima; two days later on Nagasaki. Japan was defeated.

We were met with celebrations every place we played - Erlanger, Berlin, Potsdam, Nuremberg, Munich, Heidelberg and, if you thought the names in the Pacific were difficult - try these on for size: Bad Kissinger, Bad Wildungen, Ferstenfeldbruck and Kaufbeuren.

While General MacArthur and Admiral Nimitz met with the Japanese delegation on board the USS Missouri to sign the unconditional surrender, officially signaling the end of World War II, we were flying home from Paris to celebrate in the good ol' USA.

No city was too large or town too small to rejoice in the victory. Whether it was Times Square in New York or the city square in Independence, Missouri, every man, woman and child celebrated the end of the war. It was their war. For more than four years everyone had made sacrifices to overcome the tyranny that threatened their lives; their beliefs. Ever since Plymouth Rock, we

AMERICANS HAVE BEEN WILLING TO PAY THE PRICE FOR WHAT WE
BELIEVE IN - FREEDOM.

FINALLY, WE WERE AT PEACE. A PEACE FOR WHICH WE PAID
DEARLY. BUT, NOW IT WAS TIME FOR THE RETURNING GIS TO PUT
THEIR UNIFORMS IN A TRUNK, TAKE THEIR DREAMS OUT OF MOTH
BALLS AND START LIVING AGAIN. AT ITS SIMPLEST THAT'S WHAT
WE FOUGHT FOR - THE RIGHT TO DO IT OUR WAY.

Finally... a toast to a world at peace.

I was there - wherever the hell 'there' is!